The Urb

Backyard Meat Rabbits

The Urban Rabbit Project

Boyd Craven Jr

The Urban Rabbit Project

This is a true story.

At my home.

With my family.

The names are all real.

The places are real.

Welcome to my life.

I just want to change the world.

The Urban Rabbit Project

Copyright © 2012, Boyd Craven Jr.

All Rights Reserved

No part of this publication may be reproduced in any way without the prior written consent of the author. You may not circulate this publication in any format.

The Urban Rabbit Project

Rabbits are efficient, fun to raise and they taste good too!

Rabbit is the ultimate local meat.

There have been a good many books written about raising rabbits. Most are very general and include lots of information on everything from keeping rabbits as pets, to raising rabbits for show, to breeding rabbits to sell to processors for profit. This book (Volume 1) will focus entirely on, and only on sharing with the reader our personal experiences and methods of raising rabbits on our 120'x120' city lot in Michigan as self-sufficient meat for our family.

I'm often on my soapbox in support of the argument that it's easier for a family to "need less" than to "spend more" money to buy quality food. Done our way, it costs close to zero after the initial setup is paid for. There are no taxes to pay, no middleman, no anything. It's just like we've added a meat section to our garden!

Then, just like we do with our extra tomatoes, zucchini and cucumbers from our garden, we can share or trade with our neighbors who don't have any. It's that simple. Backyard Meat Rabbits can benefit every family on the planet, in our humble opinion.

Table of Contents

Table of Contents 8

Thinking About Raising Rabbits? 9

About The Urban Rabbit Project 13

An Approaching Problem 16

Why Rabbits? 21

Where Do I Start? 26

Housing Rabbits 31

    Our Hutches 33

    Accessories 43

Feeding Rabbits 47

    Breeders 49

    Feeders 53

Breeding Rabbits 68

    When Do I Start? 70

    Breeding Day 73

    Keeping Records 75

Questions and Answers 78

Thinking About Raising Rabbits?

I am a big believer that people need to know where their food comes from, and how to obtain it without going through the drive-thru or the grocery store. It's fast becoming a lost chapter in the history of our country. It's unthinkable that our generation would allow that to happen!

Our son Boyd3 and I made the decision to learn to grow and preserve some of our own food, and are gradually getting the whole family involved. Different family members take on different roles, but the thing is, we are all reclaiming this knowledge for our family together, and are passing it on to our next generations and beyond.

We didn't know anyone raising rabbits in our area when we made our decision to get started, so we attended several public rabbit shows around the state to make contacts and to buy breeding stock. We talked to all of the "old timers" that would talk to us. In general, we found that rabbit folks are a very friendly bunch, and are glad to help someone new.

We took Boyd3's 10 year old son with us and let him get involved in the whole process. He understood that the original trio (1 buck and 2 does) would get names and be "safe". ALL of their future offspring would NOT and would be subject to our food production process.

We did in fact buy 2 does that were sisters, and just old enough to breed. We bought 1 unrelated buck that was also just old enough to breed. All 3 were Californians. We brought them and all of the stuff we were told that we would need back to my house. We let my wife Donna pick names for them, and explained the deal with the offspring to her. Suddenly, we were in the rabbit "business"!

We always approach something new with a small test, so the loss is not too great should we have a failure of some sort. We didn't have anyone to show us how to start, so we read everything we could find on the Internet on the subject.

We learned how to keep our rabbits alive in all kinds of weather, and how and when to get them to reproduce. Now it is our mission to teach anyone who wants to learn, how to get started with rabbits our way and save them from making all of the same mistakes that we made!

At first, Boyd3 and I did all of the harvesting alone. Once we "got it down", we taught his kids (my grandkids) how, and have since allowed them to participate in all of the steps in killing, skinning and gutting several litters that were ready. By the way, they had helped with feeding, watering and manure shoveling the entire time these litters grew out. Now they are learning the best ways to preserve and prepare our home harvest. I'll wait and get into all of that in detail in Volume 2, Rabbits In Jars.

One day I quietly observed two of the older teen foster girls that we had taught about our rabbits explain the whole operation to a visiting guy friend and was proud of how much they had learned, so fast. They went from "EWWWWW!!" to expert in less than a year. Now they are grown and on their own, but they took the knowledge with them.

Kids of all ages are sponges for information. Be SURE to take the time to teach them this! Do it at the "right time" for them, as they are all different. Teach them in ways that THEY can relate to as individuals. THEY are the future of our food system.

For example, as far as little ones like this are concerned, we don't eat "bunnies". We pet them. We eat "rabbits" when they get too big and scratchy. We learn how to properly hold them, what we are allowed to feed them, and how to "bunny-sit" them when the neighbors go on vacation! We learn how to plant and eat raw veggies from the rabbit garden so we know what fresh bunny food tastes like, instead of processed bunny food, and why it is better for them. Then we learn that the same thing applies to people food as well.

About The Urban Rabbit Project

The biggest thing we lacked when we started raising backyard meat rabbits was a system to follow. A priority list specific to that and what we wanted to do. We wasted lots of time, money and effort figuring out what to do and how to do it. Where to get stuff and what stuff to get! What to feed our rabbits and what not to feed them. Now that we've done that, in order to save others the hassle, I have written down EXACTLY what we do here that works well for us, as a system that others may wish to follow. It's a starting place for beginners who have nobody to teach them in person, or ideas for those looking at other reasonable, natural options.

To me, the success of this effort will not be judged by how many books are sold. It's more about how effective The Urban Rabbit Project is as a whole in teaching teachers to teach others how and why to get started raising rabbits. It's about the sharing of information, providing a place for questions and answers, and in providing a means for enthusiasts to find one another safely. A portion of sales will help to finance these.

It's incredible how much easier and how much more effective it is for the beginner to have a LOCAL go-to person available to purchase stock that's already acclimated to the local weather conditions when they're just starting out. Nobody knows better than one of the beginner's neighbors with hands-on experience how to design a natural feeding program based on what is available where they live, or what type of housing suits the rabbits AND the people's needs best.

We live in Michigan, in the United States. The plants we have available here for natural feed programs are very similar to what our friends in most other "cold weather" states have. Our housing needs are similar too. However, our friends that live say in the desert in California don't have grass, clover and dandelions in their backyards, and in fact what they have is different than our friends in Mexico or Malasia have in theirs. I can't tell them what the best plants are, because I don't even know what they have! To do THAT, this "system" needs a global network of those local go-to people, all on the same page with the basics, but armed with local experience. To accomplish that, I will (with help from others) attempt to build and maintain a Global Rabbitry List and publish it on the Internet so that you the reader may find them. It will be hosted on my domain at

www.TheUrbanRabbitProject.com

as well as on my Facebook page at

www.facebook.com/TheUrbanRabbitProject

as well as in a self-editable version in the Files area of the public discussion group/community created to complement this effort at

www.facebook.com/groups/Backyard.Meat.Rabbits/

One of the goals of this effort is to identify, or to help teach someone in every state of the United States to become one of these local "go-to people", or Rabbiteers. (A title I just made up!) Then, with their assistance we'll identify or teach someone to do the same in every county, parish, or borough of every state of the United States. That's all 3,143 of them! Then, where ever interest exists around the globe.

Together, this system and these go-to people will help solve, in advance, an approaching problem by sharing and supporting this simple, efficient way of raising rabbits in small numbers for meat and fertilizer in our backyards, that anyone can follow. You CAN provide your family with delicious, clean, almost free, natural meat!

An Approaching Problem

It has been said that there were nearly 7 billion people on the planet at the end of 2011. It is estimated that there will be over 10 billion by the year 2050. That's within the realistic and expected lifespans of many people reading this guide! There are also other changes taking place within the global population that will affect our world more than the sheer growth of our numbers will. What the "developing countries" around the world are developing the fastest is a middle class. Their people are moving away from the simple country life and into the cities, or into urban settings as close to the cities as they can in huge numbers. They want what the middle class of the United States and the other "developed" countries of the world have! They want a car. They want a house with electricity, central heating and cooling and indoor plumbing. They want grocery stores, Walmart and fast-food! Who can blame them for wanting what we have? Not me.

Their getting what we have though, and living like we live IS the approaching problem! Unless we lead by example and make some fundamental changes, the approaching problem WILL arrive. In our lifetime!

Our "developed" way of life is extremely energy dependent. For example: We simply cannot function without electricity anymore. Kill the electricity to the whole civilized world for an extended period of time and a HUGE percentage of the people would die. Civilization would fall apart. We simply no longer have the tools or the knowledge to get by without it! That's pretty scary.

Our current definition of normal life is also really fossil oil dependent. Running out of it, or getting low on it suddenly would affect our food supply system with much the same ferocity that the bursting of the real estate price bubble in 2008 in the U.S. affected everything else. We kind of knew it could happen, were kind of afraid it might happen, did nothing to prepare for it, and totally got our butts kicked when it did happen! Will we really let something like that happen to us again?

Here in the United States, our population equates to roughly 5% of the world's total, yet we use 25% of all of the world's oil. The way we produce and distribute our food is very oil/energy dependent, and very inefficient. In fact, it's getting down right ridiculous. We rely on giant corporations, farming massive amounts of land with really big, expensive, fuel guzzling machinery to grow corn and cereal grains. Then we rely on oil based transportation to take these crops to centralized mills and animal feedlots to process them. (Let's follow the meat now) Then we rely on that transportation again to take the animal to the slaughter house. We rely on electricity to keep the meat cool or frozen. Transportation again to get the meat to the distribution center. Electricity again to keep it cool or frozen. Transportation again to get the meat to the grocer or food establishment. Transportation again to get you to the grocery store. Electricity again when you get the meat home to keep it cool or frozen. Whew! Get the picture? And the rest of the world wants to be like us?? That almost sounds like a system that our government would invent! We need to cut out some of these steps, expenses and dependencies.

Regardless of oil/energy prices, or who is getting along or not getting along in the world, as the global middle class expands that much, there just isn't going to be enough oil/energy to make enough food for that many people, doing things the way we do them now, and being as inefficient as we are now. Period.

I am not, and don't want to be thought of as a "Doom & Gloomer". I am very optimistic about our future! There are some very smart people out there working on alternative fuels and renewable energy, and I believe in what they are doing. I put my money (what little of it there is) where my mouth is and invest in the stock of some of these companies. Particularly companies developing renewable, drop-in fuels that work with the stuff we already have, so we don't all have to go get new stuff! Also companies who create more electricity for the grid from clean, renewable sources. While they do this, the rest of us (hopefully) should figure out things that each of us can do to use less energy and produce more QUALITY food, more efficiently than we are now. We're smart enough, we just have to be disciplined enough do it, and lead by example! Every time we spend a dollar on food, we need to remember that that dollar is just like a vote we are casting on what type of world we want to live in!

During World War I and World War II, "Victory" gardens of fruit and vegetables were encouraged and promoted at private residences and even on public ground to reduce pressure on the public food supply and food prices. They saved fuel "for the war effort". Citizens felt a sense of accomplishment in doing what they could to help! For different reasons, we need to do that again. We can plant "Rabbit Gardens". We have one in our 120'x120' city lot. We only raise plants in it that both our rabbits and us can eat, or that we can eat with rabbit meat. By doing that, we supplement the rabbit's diet, our diet and take a big bite out of those inefficiencies that I was just talking about.

We should all re-learn how to do these things for ourselves.

Just because it makes sense. Before we have to. Then we need to teach others.

Together, we CAN make a difference!

Why Rabbits?

There are many reasons to raise backyard meat rabbits. Rabbits are, in my opinion, the ultimate in "local meat". Remember all of those steps, expenses and dependencies I mentioned earlier that need eliminating? Raising backyard meat rabbits our way takes care of ALL of them. No electricity needed!

Locavores are a group of people who practice eating food within a certain range of miles from their home. Rabbits can fit into any range, whereas most other large meat animals cannot. That makes rabbit a perfect meat choice for locavores to raise themselves, or to purchase within their community.

Some folks keep a couple of rabbits just for the awesome manure that they provide so much of! **Bunny berries** (manure) are fantastic as fertilizer for your garden, flowers and lawn. My son calls them our mobile organic fertilizer units.

Preppers, or survivalists are a large and growing group of people who believe in being "prepared" for disasters or social breakdowns resulting from natural disasters, war or financial collapse. One of the things they practice is food storage and self-sufficiency, so they'll have food if it suddenly becomes scarce for any reason. Rabbits fit perfectly into a prepper's plan. They take very little space to raise. They make almost no noise or odor to give away their location to any passers-by. If food ever did become scarce, hiding cows, pigs, goats or chickens from hungry people wanting to take yours would be difficult. You can hide a few rabbits very easily! A small pen of rabbits is like a living pantry that you can reach into one meal at a time.

Homesteaders should consider rabbits as their very first meat animal. They are on par with chickens for low start-up cost. I personally believe that rabbits are way easier to slaughter and process than chickens. They can be fed a wide variety of whatever the new homesteader has available on his/her property.

There are lots of people, like me for example, who **simply want to know what they are going to eat has been eating!** Every day lately there are scary or just plain gross stories making the news about CAFOs. (Concentrated Animal Feeding Operations) There's just nobody I trust more than me to properly feed and care for my food. I know that I'm not going to feed any antibiotics or genetically modified feed to my rabbits. They are also currently the only meat animal I'm allowed to raise where I live.

Feeding rabbits does not compete with feeding people. That's very important. It's easier to create MORE food for our growing population if we don't feed something that we can eat to something else that we can eat! Rabbits don't have to eat corn. Rabbits don't have to eat cereal grain. What rabbits CAN eat that doesn't compete is what you have in your very own backyard. Grass, dandelions and clovers. We simply need to change how we manage our properties! We can still have a pretty, manicured lawn in the front of the house for people to see, if we want to. In the backyard, that nobody sees, is where the HUGE opportunity lies. Instead of spending our money on it and damaging the environment by chemically fertilizing it, applying weed killer to it, mowing it, bagging it and sending it to the landfill, we can feed OUR rabbits with it, and in turn feed ourselves and your families with the very best tasting, best for us meat around! No pink slime. No antibiotics. No GMO's. Just exactly what nature intends for us to eat. Good, pure, wholesome, nearly free meat!

According to what I read, rabbit meat is the highest in protein, lowest in fat and calories. (I of course have no way to scientifically verify these figures)

Animal	Calories/Lb.	% Protein	% Fat
Rabbit	795	20.8	10.2
Veal	840	19.1	12
Chicken	810	20	11
Turkey	1190	20	20.1
Lamb	1420	15.7	27.7
Beef	1440	16.3	28
Pork	2050	11.9	45

Rabbit meat is also very easy to digest and is often recommended for specialty health related diets. It's just plain delicious to eat! It works in virtually any recipe that calls for chicken, but it's more dense and more filling pound for pound. It doesn't taste like chicken to me, but a lot of people compare the two. It takes on flavors and seasonings well. It works great as jerky and sausage. You may can it or freeze it safely. My preference is canning it in jars. There is a peace of mind having my meat supply shelf stable if there is ever a power outage for any reason. I've had my freezer well stocked with rabbit meat before and spent too much time worrying about the power in storms and such.

You can "harvest" them as needed, by yourself, at home, without the need for much specialized equipment.

The organ meat is high in minerals and vitamins, and makes an excellent pate, I'm told. I'm not a liver eater myself. My friends are trying to get me to try it in a gravy. They may talk me into it! I always have so much of it! For those who choose not to partake of it, (liver, kidney and heart) it makes an excellent, wholesome food for your dogs or cats.

or...

Look what Seth caught with the "secret weapon" rabbit liver bait!

Where Do I Start?

"So, where exactly do I start?" is the number one question I get asked.

"With a plan!" is always my response.

A successful backyard meat rabbit program is NOT rocket science, like some people make it out to be. Anyone can develop one. Armed with just some really basic knowledge of a few things rabbit, and MOSTLY a solid understanding of our family's eating habits, I eventually developed the perfect plan for us. I didn't do it by myself though, and I didn't do it right away. We didn't do things in this order when we started out. Let's save you that mistake!

Communication is critical to good planning here. If the person who will be actually raising the rabbits is different than the person who will normally be doing the meal planning and the cooking of the family meals, both have to be on the same page! How many meals per week, all year long will you actually prepare using rabbit meat? In our case, it's just my wife Donna and I at home now. The kids are all grown and gone. We decided that one big meal per week would be a realistic place to start. Then we had to figure out just how much meat was enough for that one big meal. In the beginning, we figured (based on what we'd read) that one fryer would make that meal for us. Everyone seemed to SAY that 5lb. young rabbits of 8 weeks old are the most tender and desirable. What we found to be true for US real quick was something different entirely!

We don't often fry any kind of meat, including rabbit. Everyone seems to start out that way. We did too. Why? I guess because we have that imprinted in our brain somewhere. The truth is, rabbit is SO lean and fat free that you have to be careful not to overcook it or dry it out when preparing it. We found that out the hard way. Eventually we got pretty good at it. By then though, we were sort of burned out on fried rabbit, so we began to bake it more often than not in liquids. That method really suited our likings better, but we always had lots of leftovers to figure out what to do with. We found ourselves pulling the meat off of the bones of the leftovers and adding it into other recipes. Soups, chilis, salads, you name it. Pretty much the same thing we've always done when we cook a whole turkey or chicken and had leftovers, only we REALLY liked this better!

So, we had one big meal of baked rabbit for the two of us and had leftover meat that we liked, but it wasn't quite enough meat really to make that second meal. It was a little on the skimpy side for the main course. Being the highly intelligent folks that we are, (big smile) we figured out the second YEAR of doing this, that a larger than 5lb. rabbit was what we needed! We grew them out a bit longer and a little bit larger, par-boiled the whole rabbit (cut up into convenient pieces) and pulled the meat off the bones right away. Then we could freeze or can the meat in pint jars. In this form, the meat was not a bit tough, as we'd been conditioned to believe, and it was really convenient. You can whip out a meal in no time when you have canned, fully cooked, deboned meat ready to go at a moment's notice! The other thing we liked about canning it, was not having to worry about the power going out and having a freezer full of rabbit to worry about.

So what the heck does all this have to do with raising rabbits? It's what you have to know before you can do that planning part I mentioned just a minute ago. This information is what made it possible to perfect our plan. Each large rabbit fills 2 of the pint jars, so 26 large rabbits will provide us with 1 meal per week. If you'll need a quart per week, double that to 52 large rabbits!

Each of my does average 8 kits per litter. I can get 5 litters per year from each. Do the math real quick, and you'll see that each of my does can produce 40 offspring that weigh in at 6+ pounds each at harvest time. (That's more than 24 times her own weight of about 10 pounds! Try that with a cow.) I don't need that many, so theoretically 1 doe would provide us with all of the meat we wanted. Theory doesn't cut it though in the real world. Stuff happens. Murphy always shows up. I always recommend breeding 2 does really close together, for reasons we'll cover later.

Having 2 does really takes the pressure off. If I breed them each only twice a season, that's 32 large rabbits, or 64 meals in pint jars. That's not too scary at all. Even if I make mistakes while learning, we can still eat that 1 meal per week of rabbit. If along the way we decide to increase the amount we want to eat, we already have the flexibility to do so. The bottom line is, 2 does can easily feed my family of two 1 good meal a week with rabbits to spare, share, or trade. I know exactly what they've eaten, and maybe more importantly what they haven't eaten. I know that they have been raised and harvested as ethically and humanely as possible. No other person has touched them during their entire life-cycle except me (and maybe the neighbor kids petting them when they're very small). No medicines or antibiotics have ever been introduced in their feed, so my family isn't eating it second hand. All this, right from my backyard, and they're so quiet nobody will ever know that they're back there. In the city! I can't do that with beef and I can't do that with poultry. Pigs are out of the question.

Once you have this part figured out, it's easy to know what you'll need, and when you will need it. In our case, we had to plan for 2 does and 1 buck.

Housing Rabbits

I was a little torn whether to cover housing or the feed program first, because you kind of have to have them both figured out a bit before you actually bring any rabbits home if you want to do it right. So I decided to talk about how I do housing first, here in Michigan. In "Feeding Rabbits" we'll get into integrating housing with feeding. Then you'll see what I mean!

You really have to know which breed you plan to raise before you know what size your housing needs to be. The 2 most popular breeds of rabbits raised for meat are New Zealands and Californians. They are larger, hardy breeds that do well outdoors. They can take cold weather much better than hot. They don't do well in wet, drafty or breezy places. They like to have a place to hide if frightened or to have their young. These are the basic requirements that must be considered when choosing how and where you'll keep them. We chose Californians. Why? We found Californians close to home. Pretty scientific, huh? Just honest. Both breeds are similar in size. Both have favorable meat to bone ratio and favorable feed conversion rates. Both need the same amount of space.

We decided to use easily movable, outdoor hutches suitable for the weather here in Michigan. They are designed to outlast the 3-5 years of breeding viability expected from our breed. Each breeder is permanently assigned their own hutch. The hutches are 3' long by 2' deep and 2' tall inside. That provides ample space for the doe and her kits until they are weaned. When the kits leave the doe's hutch, they are combined with other similar aged kits in a grazer run. (Like the picture on the cover) Once they are placed in the grazer, we quit calling them kits and start calling them feeders. Why? Real scientific, again. In the grazer, we need to keep them safe, comfortable, give them ample room for exercise and muscle toning and FEED them well, until we are ready for them. It's like adding a meat section to your kitchen garden!

Our Hutches

We found a local, Michigan craftsman who builds a good, sturdy, basic rabbit hutch with untreated wood and 1/2"x1", 14 gauge galvanized wire floors and side wire. (Never use a thinner gauge wire on the floor as it will cut the rabbit's feet.)

We paid Richard Coburn (248-673-1436) a visit and described our plans for our 4 season outdoor rabbitry. We told him our needs and what we have to work with (like the fact that we don't own a truck). He agreed to cooperate with us to modify his design. The first thing we needed was to make the legs removable with four 3" deck screws in each instead of nail gun nails, so the hutch would fit in the hatchback of my little Chevy Aveo! If a person can, it's better to build them on site. If you're building them to sell, remember this tip. Not everyone has a truck.

The original design had a fixed plywood floor in the "hide" compartment (on the left) and a fixed divider wall, with a wire floor in the main compartment. Fixed wooden floors are nearly impossible to keep clean over time. We had Richard put a 1 piece wire floor in the entire hutch. We made the divider wall removable so the hutch can be opened up in the spring for use as a buck's breeding facility/home or put back in the winter for additional shelter, with a plywood floor insert over the wire and plenty of straw to keep him warm.

The normal problem with wooden hutches is that rabbits back up into a corner of their choosing to pee. With more than one rabbit in a hutch, they choose different corners. If you have floor wire over a wooden 2x2 floor frame, that leaves a 1-1/2" lip all of the way around the inside of the hutch that stacks up with pee and poop and gets really disgusting, really quickly!

We had Richard rip 2"x2"s at a 45 degree angle and miter the corners to cover those spots. Now there is nowhere for the yuck to build up. It just runs/rolls right onto the wire and drops through. That keeps the hutch really clean inside and easy to hose out and disinfect on a regular basis.

You cannot paint/stain the inside of a hutch as the occupants will chew it off and eat it. Just raw, untreated wood. They can and will eat that, so we make each piece replaceable. Just in case. On the outside, do whatever you feel like. We chose a drab green camouflage type of outdoor paint so they kind of disappear in the bushes.

As a doe's hutch the divider wall is usually only ever removed for cleaning purposes. During the warm months, she almost always has a litter, or is near to having one, therefore building her new nest for each litter. When it's kindling time, instead of adding a nesting box, we add a simple, flat 3/8" plywood floor that lays right on top of the wire inside the hide compartment. I suppose that you could even use a couple of layers of heavy cardboard instead. Each new litter gets a fresh floor. If it gets too gross before they're done with it, we just turn it over.

As we worked on the design, we put a doe near to kindling in one, let her raise the litter in it, all the while watching for what could be improved. We built the next one with the improvement, put another doe in it and watched while she raised her litter in it. We did it again, and again, and again.

One thing that I always tell people to remember when designing a rabbit's housing is that not only must it be designed to keep the rabbit in, but it must keep predators out! Sturdy wood and wire hutches like these will withstand dog attacks, skunk and raccoon attacks. Yes, I've had all of those here within the city limits. With 1/2"x1" wire all around no large snakes or rats can get in to eat the young. Did I say that I hate snakes? We've never had a bear get after one of our hutches, but I don't think that they'd keep a bear out. I can sleep well at night knowing that my rabbits are safe inside their hutch out in my backyard.

On my next hutch design, I'm going to make all 4 walls as removable sub-assemblies, so for example if I want to change the solid wood panel on one end with a 1/2"x1" wire panel, I just unscrew it, pop it out and pop the new one in. That way I can micro-manage air flow when I have babies or not in each hutch. (It's called continuous improvement. I never quit.)

We have quite an evolutionary line-up of hutches! These are some of them.

Our current model works really well in all four seasons, in many backyards here in Michigan. It's a hutch that we've standardized to meet the needs of the rabbit that lives in it based on seasonal and litter requirements.

They need to be placed in a convenient, shady place in your backyard. Try to pick a spot for them on the north side if you can, where you can see from inside the house. Every time you hear a noise outside at first, you'll wonder if it was the rabbits, or something after the rabbits! Put them where you can easily reach them with the water hose for rinsing out. If you place them out of sight from the street, passers-by won't even know that you have rabbits back there. Believe it or not, people might actually take them if they see them. Some people may steal them for themselves, but what you really want to be aware of are the nut jobs that think that rabbits have "rights" like humans, and need to be "rescued". What a world we live in!

Another thing to keep in mind when choosing where to place your hutches is visitors. Where do you want them to be? Little kids (and big kids) love to hold and pet bunnies!

It turns out that the top loading hutches and grazers are also the best and the safest for the rabbits, the little visitors, and you by eliminating what I call "door anxiety". It's just way too easy to get some serious scratches while trying to drag a back-peddling rabbit out of a small door to handle. There's none of that with a top loader. The whole roof opens up, you reach in (or in the case of a grazer run, get in) and calmly, with both hands pick up and cuddle your rabbit. There's just no way I'll risk a scar on one of the little visitors. Their only thought is how cute and adorable the bunnies are. I aim to keep it that way. Think ahead!

After I decide on a good location for each hutch, I remove the grass and about 6 inches of soil directly below each hutch. That creates kind of a bowl and makes it easier to scoop out the "bunny berries" and keep the flies away. The urine is actually what smells the most, so if you spray the water hose under the hutch once in awhile, especially when it's hot outside, you shouldn't notice them with your nose either!

I had the idea that I would fashion a sort of chute underneath the floor wire made of 1/4"x1/4" hardware cloth so the poop would roll nice and neat into a bucket and the urine would just go straight down onto the soil, but I haven't got it perfected yet.

Why do this? 2 reasons. #1= Convenience. Easy to get the bunny berries where you want them without doing a bunch of unnecessary work with a shovel. #2= "Clean" bunny berries. Separate little balls that are easy to pour, or dry in the sun. Some people turn feed bags inside out and refill them with bunny berries to sell to others in bulk to help offset feed costs. I have plans of grinding dried bunny berries in a burr grinder into a coffee grounds consistency. That would fill a nice sprinkle can for naturally fertilizing anything from flowers, to vegetables, to lawns, you name it, more covertly than having raw, round ones lying all over. It would make even more perfect worm food for a worm bin than the plain bunny berries would. It'd make awesome Bunny Berry Tea Bags (a business venture in the works) for dropping in your water can well before watering your favorite whatevers. Rabbit manure is valuable stuff. So far I've used all of mine myself in my garden, my dad's garden or my son's garden. Soon, I'm going to sell some of it like I mentioned above at local farmers markets, packaged nice and pretty like, so it doesn't look "dirty"!

Accessories

Now that you have your hutches in place, before you bring any rabbits home there are still a few more things that you need to have. This is where it can get confusing and you can spend a whole bunch of money that you just don't need to. What you are going to need for sure are containers for food and water. After much research and more than a few dumb purchases we settled on 20oz. Plastic EZ-Crocs that fasten to the inside of the wire on the front of the hutch. The croc has to be held in place or the rabbit will spill it all immediately. It should be easy to remove (like every time you're out there) so you can dump it, rinse it, replace it and refill it. You just can't teach them not to poop in their water croc. They can't poop in a water bottle it's true, but when it gets cold outside and the water gets hard (freezes), one tap on something solid knocks the ice out of a croc so easily. You can also bring a croc into the house and throw it in the dishwasher on a regular schedule. I find cleaning bottles and nipples a pain. I go for the easy way. They cost about $4 each. I have 2 for each hutch. One in use, another being cleaned. I guess if you had a bunch you'd only need a few spares.

To fill the crocs I just save a plastic gallon milk jug, fill it with water, go out there to the hutches and pour right through the wire. I don't even have to lift the lid if the croc is clean and just needs filling. Saving steps in nasty weather makes all of the difference in the world.

Occasionally the water crocs will develop stains and some algae. A good trick to know for cleanup is that pouring white vinegar inside them mixed with water, then letting them soak for a couple of hours before washing them will loosen the stains right up.

For the pellet feeder I bought 5-1/2" plastic EZ-Feeders by the same company. They cost about $5 each. I have 1 for each hutch. They are actually the model designed to mount on the front wire too with the filler neck on the outside and the feed cup on the inside. That requires cutting a small hole in the wire, but leaves the filler neck exposed to the elements. Wet feed is no good, so I mount them inside the hutch on the back wall with 1 screw.

The other thing you see in this picture is a plastic resting mat designed to clip into floor wire. They provide relief to the rabbit from the wire, while still allowing poop to pass through. They are easy to clean, and require no tools. They cost about $1.50 each. I have 1 for each hutch.

I ordered all 3 of these accessories online at www.klubertanz.com and they shipped them right to my door.

Feeding Rabbits

The most important thing to know about feeding is that all of your rabbits should have as much fresh, clean water as they can drink at all times. They should NEVER run dry of water. Rabbits fed with pellets won't even eat without enough water available.

Feeding the right rabbits the right diet, at the right time, in the correct amounts for their age and their "purpose" is the second most important thing that you need to learn.

Just about everyone, when getting started raising rabbits starts off feeding them commercial rabbit feed pellets. You can buy them in various sized bags from 1 pound to 50 pounds. The bigger the bag you buy, the better the price per pound you get. You can raise your rabbits on pellets and water and nothing else. They contain everything your rabbits need to stay alive and grow, including the proper ratios of fiber, protein and minerals. They are also the object of attention to every backyard Rabbiteer that I know.

As soon as the beginner gets comfortable with all of the various aspects of raising rabbits, and maybe even before, a light bulb goes off in their head that tells them that there are potential problems with feeding your herd this way. First, you cannot control the quality of the ingredients going into the pellet recipe. You can read the label, but do you understand it? Are the ingredients natural, or GMO? Were they ever sprayed with pesticides or fertilized in an unnatural way? We don't really know for sure, do we? Isn't this one of the biggest reasons we decided to raise our own meat in the first place? We wanted to be sure of what they are eating.

I divide my feeding program into 2 parts. Breeders and Feeders. The breeders are going to "make" what you're going to eventually eat, and "set the stage" for what the feeders are going to eat, but are one step removed because you will not be eating them. You want to always remember that what the feeders eat, so will you eventually. Good stuff in, good stuff out! They are what they eat and all that.

Breeders

Your breeders are where you should first focus your attention and your money. Feeding them well should be priority one in whatever budget you allow for your rabbitry. They are your workforce and your raw materials. Their condition is what determines the quality and the quantity of your finished product.

Happy breeders seem to be the best candidates for healthy breeders, in my opinion. Rabbits can get bored of eating the same old thing all of the time. They like something to chew on and they like a little variety in their diet. Just like people, if rabbits eat too many easy calories, they'll get fat. If they eat too many pellets out of boredom and are not pregnant or nursing they'll get fat. You have to limit the amount of pellets based on the weight of the rabbit. Directions should be on the label of the feed bag, and vary by ingredients of the pellet recipe. A good rule of thumb is ½ to 1 ounce of pellets for each pound the rabbit weighs daily. I feel their back. If I can feel their bones very much, I go more towards the 1oz ration. If I can hardly feel any bones at all, more towards the ½ oz ration. 1 cup of pellets by volume is about 5-1/2 ounces by weight. If you can, feeding them ½ of their ration in the morning and ½ of their ration at dusk is best. Try to be consistent with whatever schedule that you can manage.

Feeding your doe unlimited pellets during the last week of pregnancy and the next 4 weeks after insures her getting enough of the right nutrients and calories for her body to do what it needs to do. She won't get fat then. Pellets are highly densified and dried. It's the easiest way of getting extreme amounts of nutrients in her. Remember, she's supplying the needs of usually 8 or more developing babies in there. She can't spend all day eating, she needs rest. She also needs more water than usual. The dried feed will absorb liquids like crazy and expand. Without huge amounts of water, she'll get dangerously dehydrated. Have you ever eaten a bunch of dehydrated bananas, or fruit, then got a belly ache? Same thing, only rabbits cannot vomit. They'll die!

This part is IMPORTANT to my feeding program. I grow out ALL of my feeders in grazer runs, eating ONLY what is in my backyard, or that which I forage easily. To have the doe set the stage for that, I feed her some of what the feeders will eventually get every day. That way while they are developing inside her, she's eating it. After her litter is born, I keep feeding it to her, so they are getting it from her milk while nursing.

After 10 days or so the babies eyes are open and soon they'll wander around the hutch exploring. In the pictures you'll notice that I place the pellet feeder right by the door of the nest. They'll start nibbling on the pellets first. I place some of their eventual natural food on the far side of the hutch, so they can get a taste of it right away. This is considered very controversial by most of the books out there. Most of them say that you can't feed anything raw and green to a young rabbit until 6 months old. Well, my feeders will be in my belly, or in a jar WAY before 6 months, so I developed this method on my own. Try it at your own risk, but I have NEVER lost a single kit by carefully doing this! They don't eat much at first, but after about 4 weeks they're eating machines! I constantly increase the amount of natural food they receive during the course of the 4-6 weeks they're with mom. This is where the purpose thing I mentioned earlier comes in. It's a proven fact that the longer the kits remain with mom nursing AND eating both pellets and greens, the faster they will get to 5 pounds (the normal harvest weight). Thinking about it though, it's easy to see that the longer they stay, the fewer numbers you can get out of each doe each year. Each Rabbiteer will have to weigh the facts and decide which method to choose. I personally don't care how long it takes the feeders to get to 5 pounds or more, because their feed doesn't cost me anything once they're in the grazer run. I also happen to believe that rabbits raised on backyard pasture taste better than rabbits raised on pellets.

When her litter leaves her, the doe continues to eat pellets and greens, but you have to go back to controlling the amounts if she's not already pregnant again. She'll gain too much weight if allowed to continue on unlimited pellets when she's not. That will lead to breeding and kindling problems, besides the obvious health related problems from obesity.

Feeders

If you're raising rabbits for your table, your feeding program determines your cost per pound for your meat. If you plan to sell them, in any form, it determines the price you need to sell them for to make a profit. Your feeding program is really the only ongoing cost involved, and drives everything else!

It's really convenient to just open a 50# bag of pelleted feed from the local feed store and just fill up everybody's dish, every day. They'll survive and thrive on nothing else, but it's not very economical, and it HAS to be very boring for them that way. In fact, over the last 50 years, rabbits have actually been bred for exactly that. The rabbits are designed for pelleted feed and the pelleted feed is designed for the rabbits! A lot of research has gone into formulating exactly what ingredients go into the diet a breeding doe needs to keep her fit as she produces and nurses 5 litters per year. It's not, however the same diet a feeder needs from weeks 5 until whenever..

Most big indoor commercial growers feed nothing but pellets and water, every day. That's cleaner and requires less space and less labor, but it jacks the price way up because pellets aren't cheap. In early 2010 I was buying 50# for $10. By late 2012 the same exact thing was $15. That is why when you can find rabbit at the grocery store, it's usually frozen, and VERY expensive compared to chicken, fish and some cuts of red meat. It doesn't have to be that way. It sort of depends on how much effort you want to put into feeding them. Do it right, and other than about 3 weeks of pellets per litter, it can be free!

Boy, am I gonna get tore up by pellet manufacturers and feed stores for pointing this out, but it's true! Think about it. Rabbits have been around for WAY longer than pelleted feed. So they must have eaten something, right?

Feeders will grow way faster on pellets than backyard pasture, but backyard pasture is free! That's why I wean them from nursing and put them in their own grazer run at 5 weeks. I supplement them with pellets as they learn to graze, gradually decreasing the amounts of pellets each day until they are 100% on backyard pasture and "extras" I cut & carry from the garden, etc.

I build a 4'x8' bottomless grazer run with ½" x ½", 19 gauge galvanized hardware cloth sides and corrugated PVC panel top and let them eat grass, dandelions and clover right in my backyard!

Of course I NEVER use pesticides, weed killer, chemical fertilizer or anything else in the backyard. I also intentionally add white clover seed and I let the dandelions grow. The rabbits will actually eat them first! I just move the grazer run a couple of times a day and they are quite happy. If I leave rabbits over 4 months old in the same place for too long, they will eventually dig their way out of a bottomless grazer, but if I put 5 week old feeders in one, move it a couple of times a day, I have never had them dig out. Even if they do somehow escape, mine have always stayed right around the yard until caught with a long handled fishing net, or as a last resort, the pellet gun.

There are numerous benefits to using grazers exclusively for growing out feeders. I find the cost of housing per rabbit to be cheaper than anything else I've tried. It's also a very flexible housing. I can constantly add or subtract from the population with loosely similarly aged rabbits. If I have 6 ten week old rabbits currently in one grazer and need a home for 8 six week old rabbits from a different litter, I can do it in a grazer. I simply put the six week olds in a wire cage with food and water and place the whole thing inside the grazer for a few days. The usual butt sniffing, posturing and general getting acquainted process still takes place, but the littler ones are protected by the wire walls of their cage, so they are not injured. After the few days are up, I release them into the general population and remove the wire cage. Everybody is already used to everybody, so the danger of a size difference is eliminated. Less accessories are needed in a grazer as compared to a hutch or cage. For one, no feeders. The ground IS the feeder. No feeders to buy, no feeders to clean. Believe it or not, rabbits drink less water when eating fresh greens, as the greens themselves are by percentage mostly water. Therefore, less labor carrying water, less watering equipment to buy or to clean. Labor is reduced greatly when it comes to cleaning under hutches, cages or cleaning pans. They just spread their waste evenly in a path as wide as the grazer as it moves, then it quickly disappears into the grass. That brings another savings to mind. Cost of fertilizer and labor to spread it. Again, the rabbits do it for you. No extra charge. You may have to fill in some minor holes that they dig, but the surrounding grass roots will quickly expand into it and regrow the grass. I take the opportunity to sow some perennial white clover seed just behind the grazer's path occasionally while the grass is short and the soil is aerated well. Another benefit that is not as obvious is the improved texture of the actual meat. With plenty of room to run, jump and generally have a blast, the toning of the muscles is even more perfect for cooking low and slow without turning it to mush. All in all, the rabbits condition their own environment for constant improvement!

I have a red maple tree and a weeping willow tree in my backyard. I give trimmings and leaves from both every day to all of the rabbits as a treat, and to give them something to chew besides their grazer or hutch. I trim the next door neighbor's 2 willow trees for my rabbits too! They eat new growth willow branches up to as thick as a pencil, completely along with all of the leaves on it. All I have to do is lift the corner of the grazer's lid and toss the stuff in.

I plant fast growing greens like radishes and turnips right by the rabbits and toss them some of those every day in season. They actually prefer the radish greens over the root, so I pick them as soon as the greens are ready and just reseed them right away as I work down the row. Radishes are ready in about 21 days. Turnips take 45 days to establish, but then I just snip off the outer leaves and let the plant keep growing. They'll grow even after the first few snows before giving up. Then I pull up the root before the ground freezes hard. I keep them dry but don't let them freeze and they'll last for a few months. Your rabbits will eat them during the snowy months when there are no fresh greens available. The seeds for both are cheap if you buy in bulk.

Our rabbits love kale and Swiss chard. Both are cool weather plants that can be put in as early as the ground can be worked in the spring, and will continue growing until they finally are killed off by freezing in the winter. There are warnings about anything in the cabbage family of plants being too gassy for rabbits. At my house, again in moderation, my rabbits eat them. Rabbits can handle most things that are introduced to their diet gradually. A couple of stems from the outside of the chard, or the bottom of the kale plant daily for each rabbit. The plant keeps replacing them all year. I plan to plant an extra 4 kale plants for each breeder in our herd next spring, so their offspring can have even more. I plan to experiment with drying them in a solar dehydrator for the off season feed mix too.

We love grape tomatoes. I always plant WAY too many. I take chances by getting them in real early and play games with covering them to keep them late in the season. They thrive in raised beds full of rabbit poop. Last year I had 12 plants that got over 6 feet tall! We eat them fresh, cook with them, freeze them and dehydrate them. All the while feeding them to the rabbits too! They ADORE grape tomatoes. Go figure. They have red chests all garden season from tomato juice dripping down! Most of the books say not to feed the plants or leaves to rabbits. Because tomatoes are of the nightshade family, they claim that the plant is poisonous to rabbits. Me? I question everything. I watched escapees (it happens) eat the plants with great gusto. I caught them, and watched them. They didn't die. So, as I do when testing a questionable food, I separated a feeder from the rest and gave it just a bit. The next day more. The next day even more. It didn't die, or even have diarrhea. Myth busted, for me. Do I recommend this practice for everyone? I really can't, but I do it!

Last year I grew a twenty foot row of Sudan grass as a test. It grows so fast I could hardly believe it! It looks much like a corn plant with no corn ears and a skinny stalk. It got about 8 feet tall. I'd cut 1 stalk per rabbit each day at first, about knee high to me. I never ran out all year! The stuff regrows about 2 inches a day after you cut it, and the rabbits LOVE it. I got to where I'd just cut a handful and bend it in thirds and give it to them. They always greeted it teeth first! Good test. That one's a keeper. Are you getting the pattern? I'm not as young as I used to be, and I look for stuff that doesn't require as much bending over. :-)

Any kitchen scraps that are not meat or dairy my feeders get. Peelings and ends from all veggies, stale bread, cereal, pizza crusts, left over pasta (without meat), etc. You'll get people that will tell you that bread isn't good for them in large quantities, long term. That may be so, but they LOVE it, it puts weight on them, and my feeders only have a 7-10 week life expectancy once they hit the grazers. I regularly buy whole garbage bags of out dated bread from a local distributor for $2 a bag! There's like 15 loaves or packages of buns in each bag. The rabbits like it better the harder it gets! I just don't feed them anything moldy.

Hay is something that your rabbits should have available whenever they are in a hutch. (When they're in a grazer you don't have to worry about it!) Hay provides crude fiber to keep everything moving through the rabbit properly. They can eat as much of it as they want. You can buy it by the bag at your local feed store, if money is no object to you. You can buy it by the bale from a local farmer for like $4 per bale. That's quite a bit better. (Not straw, hay. They're different. Straw is used for bedding.) You can make your own for free. Yep. The same stuff that they are eating while in the grazer run can be cut with a lawn mower with the bagger on. Spread a dark tarp on the driveway. Dump the bagger out on it, spread it out and let it dry in the sun. Turn it and stir it around occasionally until it's fairly dry. One full good sunny day usually does it. Pack the dry grass hay into a laundry basket with lots of holes for circulation. Stack identical baskets full on top of each other, letting the weight of the top ones compress the bottom ones. After setting for a while, take the top ones off and fill the bottom ones again where they have settled. Keep dry and save for when the weather is not so nice. To get more efficient than that, you'd have to make your own pellets, and we can even talk about that in a later Volume.

Yard not big enough to pasture rabbits on and make grass hay? No problem. Find a neighbor who hasn't sprayed anything on their lawn and mow it! Churches, schools, you name it! I have NEVER had someone tell me no to mowing their grass for free. I even look at the medians on the expressway and think, rabbit feed! I know, I'm obsessed. So I've been told. I'm just saying...

The mower/bagger is your friend! You can do some pretty awesome blending of free ingredients just by mowing whatever is on the ground, dumping it out and mowing it again to chop it up fine. Twigs, leaves, weeds you toss out of the flower beds, you name it. I pile it up, get a chair in the shade, and make molasses feed blocks with it.

I mix whatever I have in a 5 gallon plastic pail, adding a 50/50 mixture of feed grade molasses and water a little at a time until it's pretty moist. Next I pack it in 6" plastic planters with my fist, pressing very hard.

You can tell that these feeders know what I've done!

After letting it set in the sun for a few minutes, I turn it out of the "mold" onto the bucket lid as a serving/carrying platter. (See all of the variety of clippings, chips and chunks stuck together and flavored by the vitamin rich molasses?)

They know what to do with it next. Here's just a bit of evidence of that! One note here. I do not make this up much in advance. I'm quite sure that it would get moldy after a few days. I never let mine eat any of this over 2 days old. (not that there's usually anything left of it after an hour or two in a grazer full of feeders.) These pictures were taken during the hot, dry spell we had here in Michigan in summer 2012.

Also, when you're cutting grass in the spring or summer for hay, before drying it, throw big handfuls right into the grazer or hutch. They love it. That's called green-chop, or cut-and-carry. They can eat as much as they want. The more they eat, the faster they grow. It takes about 4 pounds of food to make 1 pound of rabbit (for feeders). That's actually a great conversion rate! We normally harvest them as soon as they reach 5 or 6 pounds (unless we need them first). After that, the conversion rate slows way down. That means roughly 20 pounds of feed per rabbit. Buying pellets at $15 for 50 pounds, that makes pellets 30 cents a pound. $6 of feed per feeder if you buy it, or ZERO if you work at it. You choose!

In the fall, I go out and mow enough grass/fallen leaves with the push mower to fill the bag full, then dump it in a grazer of feeders. They love that mix. Instead of mowing the yard all at once, I mow a little every day for fresh feed. It works well. Free feed is a good thing!

After the grass is mowed I rake up freshly fallen leaves while they are still mostly green. Straight into a grazer they go. No leaf bags used here! Even neighbors who's lawn I cannot use because of their use of fertilizers or weed killers in the spring/summer don't add those in the fall, so their leaves are fair game too. Nobody in their right mind will refuse to allow you to rake their leaves and cart them off! You can do a great service for the elderly, your church, your school, etc. and cart it back home to feed your feeder rabbits! Everyone will be sure that you're nuts as hell, but hey, who cares?!!

At the end of garden season I clean out the annual plants gradually and carry them to the grazers. I compost the plants through the gut of the rabbits and still get to use them again back in the garden or in the lawn. Nothing goes to waste. The secret to it is to do it gradually. A few spent green bean plants and a few weeds from the edges. Some way-over-ripe tomatoes with part of the vine (small amounts for me). The remains of the broccoli plants. Stalks, leaves, everything. Squash vines. Cucumber vines. Any annual plant that is going to die and rot anyway, I pull entirely and toss in a grazer.

In the fall, I cut-back our lilac bushes a bunch. All of it goes into the grazers. The Russian Sage used for decoration gets cut-back and tossed in them too. The ornamental weeping cherry tree gets evened up at the bottom. Same thing. See how I approach this? I make sure that every single living plant that I plant on my property can in some way help support my rabbits biggest habit. Eating!

I really only feel limited on how many pounds of rabbit meat I can produce each season now by how much free food I can provide for them! At the end of the garden season here in Michigan, shortly after the snow begins falling and the free feed starts getting scarce, it's off to freezer camp with everybody, whatever their size, except the does I have chosen as breeders for next season, and my buck. If you live in a cold winter state like Michigan, you're going to have to feed next year's breeders and your buck, if you have one, from the grass hay and root vegetables that you stored up, or with pellets. Probably a combination. The better you plan, the less over-wintering in a non-productive time period will cost you. Remember, that figures into your yearly profit or loss too! Everything is driven by the feed. Before you ever get your first rabbit, give a lot of thought to how you'll feed them!

Breeding Rabbits

Domesticated rabbits reproduce like crazy! There's no need for artificial insemination supplies like most of the beef cattle industry uses or for incubation equipment like the poultry industry has. There's no shipping boxes of fertile eggs or chicks around either, as is done commonly with poultry raising. With my rabbits, I pretty much have to keep my buck separated from my does, or they ARE gonna do it! There's no waiting for the does to come into heat or waiting until any special season. Does can get pregnant pretty much any day of the year.

I COULD breed my rabbits all 12 months of the year, but I don't. For one thing, I don't like pushing them that hard. For another, I simply don't need to. I find it's much more convenient as well as much more efficient to time the growing out of my first bunch of feeders with the garden season here in Michigan. Early in spring, when everything starts turning green, the grass is beginning to need mowing, the trees are getting leaves, and my first early plants like radishes, turnips and kale start poking up in my garden is when I want the first 2 litters to be born. (Remember, the feed drives everything!)

Notice I said 2 litters. Remember earlier I mentioned having at least 2 does, even though 1 could in theory produce the numbers I want? It's so they can "back each other up". With rabbits, if something unexpected happens to a doe or a litter, it's easy to foster kits from doe #1 to doe #2 if #2 has kits of her own that are close to the same age. She'll nurse them and allow them to snuggle in with hers just as if they were her own.

Say for example I had only 1 doe. She had a litter early in the morning. The first 7 were fine. She kindled right in the perfect nest she'd made, and covered them with fur she'd pulled from her belly, just like her instincts tell her to. The 8th kit however got stuck in the birth canal, she couldn't get it out and she died. The other 7 would die too, and my breeding program would be a total loss. I'd have to either buy another doe old enough to breed, or buy a young one and lose a season waiting for her to mature. Both are unacceptable. If I had another doe that already had a litter close in age, had one the same day, or even had one within 12 to 24 hours, I could just add the other seven to hers, and she would nurse them too. The breeding program would survive. Think of the second doe as insurance. If something happened to my buck and my does were already pregnant, I'd have up to 2 months to locate another buck to buy, or make arrangements for stud service from someone else's buck. It's less critical.

When Do I Start?

I get out my calendar and decide when I want my first litter of the season to be born. For me, in my backyard here in Michigan, that perfect day is usually April 1. Why April 1? Those April showers that bring May flowers also do away with the rest of the snow and ice and start greening up the grass that the first bunch of feeders will begin to eat at 5 weeks old on May 6. (Remember, the feed drives everything.) My does kindle (give birth) at 31 days after breeding almost every time, so I back up on the calendar 31 days from April 1 to March 1, and that is my #1 does first breeding date of the year. On the 27th day after breeding, I set up the nesting area. 5 weeks after the litter is born, it goes into a grazer. Those 5 items are written on the 2013 calendar like this.

I write "Breed doe #1" on March 1.

I write "Doe #1 unlimited pellets" on March 23.

I write "Doe #1 nesting box" on March 28.

I write "Doe #1 kindle" on April 1.

I write "Wean litter" on May 6.

I skip a day after breeding doe #1 before breeding doe #2 to my buck. Repeating the same pattern on the calendar for her, the same 5 items are written on the 2013 calendar like this.

I write "Breed doe #2" on March 3.

I write "Doe #2 unlimited pellets" on March 25.

I write "Doe #2 nesting box" on March 30.

I write "Doe #1 kindle" on April 3.

I write "Wean litter" on May 8.

So there is how I plan one breeding cycle. If all goes as planned, that will yield us 16 feeders to grow out to whatever size we want on free feed from our property. In our case, one more cycle will produce another 16, bringing us past our goal of 26, so there is no huge hurry to breed them again. When we do, we have to be sure we'll have enough free feed available and enough housing and accessories to outfit them. We do however want to fit all of our litters in during the duration of the garden season. Should one wish to get as many litters as possible from this scenario, one could rebreed the does 3 weeks after they kindle. That way when the kits from the first litter are 5 weeks old and go to their own grazer, she would still have 2 weeks until the 2nd litter is due to rest and regain her condition. Some people call it closer than that even. You can plan out your entire year, just like that and adjust if there are any variations.

Those are the major 6 components of planning. Housing, feeding, breeding, housing, feeding and jars! Make sure you plan for enough of each.

What we actually do here on our city lot is more like 60-80 per season. We worked our way up to it as we went. These days we need more than one pint of rabbit per week for meals, and we can't possibly make as much rabbit jerky as everyone wishes we would!

Breeding Day

I always, always, always bring the doe to the buck's hutch for breeding. A doe will defend her domain from intruders, so if I were to take the buck to her's she'd probably attack and possibly injure him. It's best done in his 2'x3' hutch with food, water dish and divider wall all removed. Just the clean wire floor.

The very best time to start is early in the morning. Upon placing the doe in there, without any distractions, the buck should almost immediately mount her from behind. I step back a couple of steps, but remain where I can still see them. If she is receptive and he has any experience (and any aim), round 1 will be over in about 15 seconds with the buck grunting and actually falling over backwards or sideways. If he doesn't, he didn't ejaculate and breeding was NOT successful. If he does, I leave her in there for 4 rounds. (About 2-3 minutes). Then I take her back to where she came from. If she absolutely refuses him, I put her back and go get doe #2. About 8 hours later, I bring the same doe back that was successfully bred earlier for rounds 5-8. Same everything as round 1-4. The reason is, the doe produces eggs upon sexual contact from the buck. So, I want him to leave his contribution several times before AND several times after she produces the eggs. This method has proven highly successful for me, and consistently produces big litters. I let him rest for a day before calling on his services again, to allow him to get his sperm counts back up again.

A doe that just won't "lift" for him may need to be "posed" if she is a first timer. Just gently hold her head still with one hand and slide the other hand under her belly and lift her rear a couple of inches while leaving him enough room to approach from behind. This usually only has to be done once and she gets the idea. Rarely does it have to be done at all. I keep notes on each doe, and whether or not she is an easy breeder is one thing I look for. More about this in the next chapter, "Keeping Records".

A buck that "gives up" too easily or isn't interested in the chase at all is usually too fat and out of shape or too old. I exercise my buck by letting him run around in an empty grazer when I'm out in the yard. I do the same thing with my does one at a time also. Sometimes they seem to appreciate a break from their litter for a bit!

A doe that simply refuses to breed, ever, goes well with potatoes and carrots! It's just not worth the aggravation to deal with an uncooperative breeder. I immediately replace them.

Keeping Records

Record keeping is an important part of being efficient and being effective at raising backyard meat rabbits. Whether or not a person chooses to keep formal pedigrees for each of their breeders is strictly up to them. It is absolutely not required. I personally do not keep up pedigrees. I also do not tattoo my rabbits with identification in their ears. I'm only producing what meat we want for ourselves, so I have only a handful of rabbits. I identify ours simply by name (if they have one) or cage numbers if they don't. IF a person had 20-30-50 or more rabbits, they would probably HAVE to tattoo ears and label cages/hutches, just for record keeping purposes, if nothing else.

What I tend to keep track of in my breeders is some of the same stuff on a pedigree, but very informal.

Name/cage number

Parents

Date of birth

Notes

The first three are obvious. The forth item is simply anything I want to remember about that particular rabbit.

Is she easy to breed, or does she resist?

Does she build a good nest at the proper time?

Does she actually have her kits in the nest, or scatter them all over the wire?

How many kits per litter each time born.

How many days gestation each time

How many survived until harvest?

Has she failed on any of the above, and on "one more chance" before being culled?

Does she waste food by sorting?

Is she friendly to visitors, or aggressive?

Is she a biter? (I won't keep a biter)

Do I want to try breeding her to a specific buck next time for some reason?

Do I have any specific plans for her?

See, it's just common sense stuff. I can't be sure to remember all these things anymore, so I write them down on a page for each rabbit. I do all this on my computer as a simple text file. That's just me. A person could just as easily have a piece of notebook paper for each rabbit and simply add to it.

Questions and Answers

There's very little chance that I remembered to cover everything that I wanted to here in this Volume. There will always be new things learned to be shared with all. There will always be peers who have differing opinions or more suitable information for a particular question. The discussion Group on Facebook with the same name as this Volume was created and opened up to the public a little before this book was released. It is a great place to ask questions of others, pitch in and help teach others, show off pictures of your rabbits, get ideas, meet people local to you with rabbits or just socialize with other rabbit nuts whom you're sure you'll never meet!

www.facebook.com/groups/Backyard.Meat.Rabbits/ is free for anyone to join, whether they have this book or not. You'll find a friendly and growing community there, governed by a volunteer moderator team second to none. Unfriendly people or animal rights nut cases don't last long there before they are removed, rest assured. The name kind of sets the stage. Not many people get there and join by accident, thinking it's something else. Come on by and visit!

You're welcome to follow our journey with all things rabbit at www.facebook.com/TheUrbanRabbitProject or our own domain at www.TheUrbanRabbitProject.com

This has been Volume 1 of The Urban Rabbit series. Don't miss any of the other Volumes, past or future! Check the address below for an updated list:

theurbanrabbitproject.com/books/backyard-meat-rabbits/

Made in the USA
Lexington, KY
30 March 2014